Perspectives
Preventing Diseases
What Are the Issues?

Series Consultant: Linda Hoyt

Flying Start
to Literacy

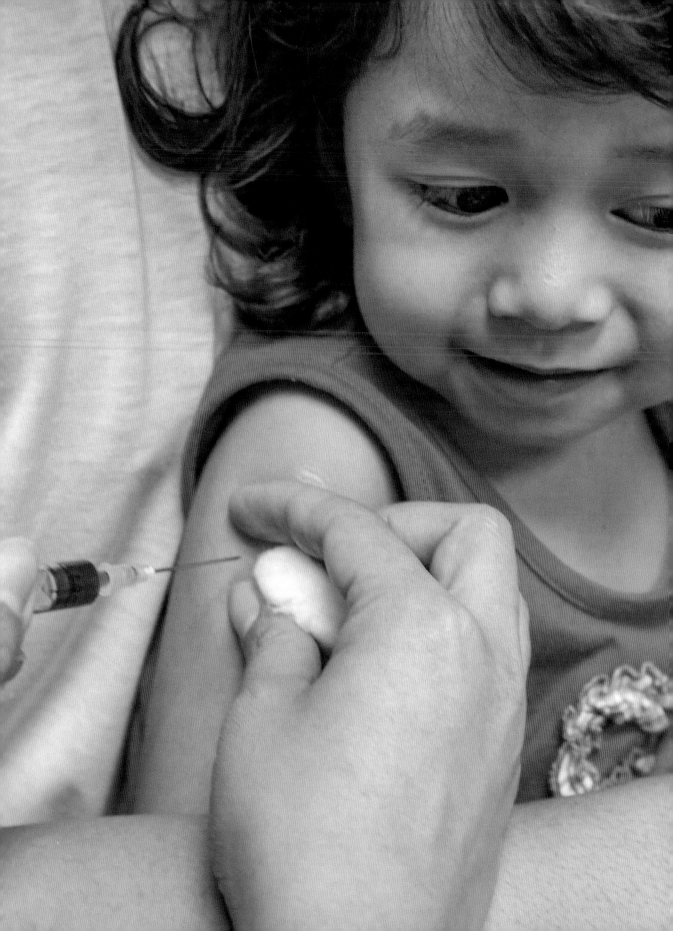

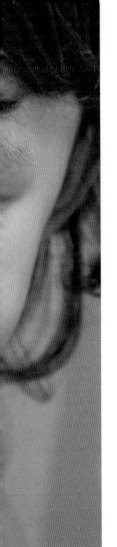

Contents

Is vaccination important?

Vaccinations help prevent diseases. They stimulate the immune system so the body is able to fight a disease if a person becomes infected.

But statistics suggest that for various reasons some people are choosing not to be vaccinated and not to vaccinate their children.

What do you think about vaccinations? Do you agree that vaccination is important? And if so, do you understand why it is important? What is your perspective?

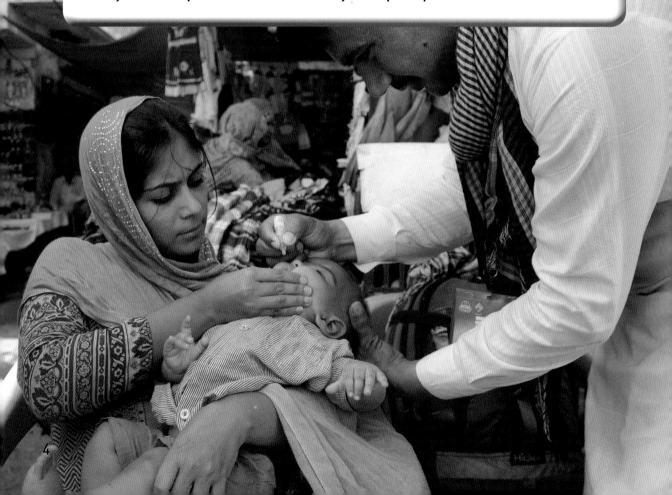

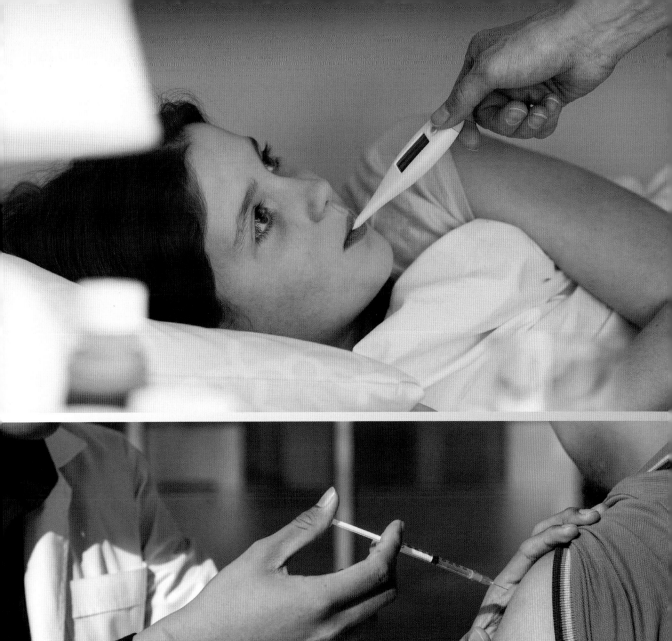

A world without polio

The United Nations International Children's Emergency Fund (UNICEF) was established in 1946 to meet the emergency needs of children. Today, UNICEF works in 192 countries around the world.

This article documents the important work UNICEF is doing today to eradicate polio.

Why is the work of UNICEF so particularly important?

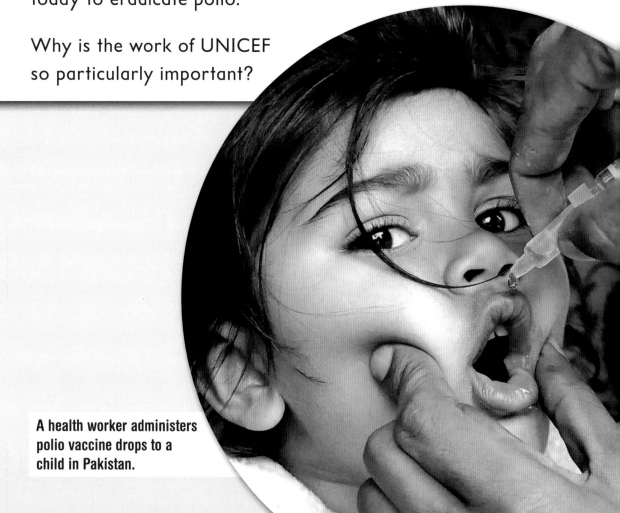

A health worker administers polio vaccine drops to a child in Pakistan.

Most kids cringe at the thought of going to the doctor for an injection. But injections do serve an important purpose. Most are vaccines, which prevent diseases and illnesses that can cause sickness or even death.

For many children around the world, immunisations are not a routine part of childhood. In poor countries where vaccines are not readily available, many children die from diseases that could have been prevented. UNICEF is one organisation working to make sure that children all around the world are protected.

Health workers prepare the polio vaccine for distribution in northern Nigeria.

UNICEF hopes to wipe out the disease known as polio. Today, thanks to the global effort to eradicate polio, much of the world is already polio-free. However, the disease is still a threat in Afghanistan, Nigeria and Pakistan.

Every year, UNICEF organises National Immunisation Days, during which as many children as possible in a country are vaccinated. In 2015, more than 172 million children in India were vaccinated on such a day. Over a five-day period in March 2015, about 5.8 million children in Iraq were vaccinated.

In 2015, 74 new cases of polio were reported. Although UNICEF is close to achieving its goal of a world without polio, it says that it must act now to wipe out the disease.

"There is no question that progress to end polio is real and tangible," said Reza Hossaini, head of Polio at UNICEF. "But – and it's a big but – until all children everywhere are consistently and routinely immunised against polio, the threat is there. We cannot let down our guard; we have to keep going until there is not a single child unvaccinated anywhere."

A group of children eagerly holding up their newly updated vaccination cards in northern India.

Measles keep Kelcey away from school

Kelcey Roberts lives in New Zealand. Her story shines a light on the importance of why we should all be vaccinated. Not just to help ourselves, but to help others in our community that can't be protected.

If you were Kelcey, what would you say to people who are able to be vaccinated, but choose not to?

Having just missed a year of school through illness and chemotherapy, 10-year-old Kelcey Roberts had just returned to school when the 2011 measles outbreak started there.

"We couldn't believe our bad luck," Kelcey's mother Tracey says. "We suddenly discovered that there were a large number of unimmunised children at Kelcey's school. That meant the odds were increased that Kelcey could contract measles – a disease that could kill her."

An electron microscopic image of a single virus particle that can cause measles.

Kelcey was diagnosed with acute lymphoblastic leukemia in December 2009. The treatment for her cancer, which reduced her immunity to very low levels, meant she was unable to attend school in 2010, except for very brief periods. She also had time off school in early 2011 and was just settling into the second semester when the first case of measles in the area was confirmed. The Roberts family were contacted by the school and Kelcey was immediately removed.

Tracey says her daughter finds it hard to fathom why other children aren't protected against a disease that could be so dangerous for people like her.

"Kelcey understands why she can't go to school because of a low blood count or when she is unwell, but she was feeling great and she couldn't go because so many students at the school hadn't been immunised."

Kelcey was away from school for five weeks during the measles outbreak. When she went back, she was restricted just to her class because of the increased risk of mixing with unimmunised children in other classes.

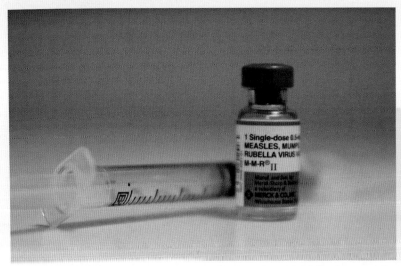

This bottle contains a measles vaccine. Doctors encourage vaccination as the best way to prevent the spread of measles.

"The local doctor called us every Wednesday to give us an update on the measles outbreak. That way, we knew when it was safer for Kelcey to go back to school," Tracey says.

"Every time I take Kelcey out of the house, it's a risk – we cannot go to the mall, the movies or places with lots of people. Measles can live on surfaces for two hours. There was one case of a child with measles who went to the movies, and there was a risk they could have spread it to other children."

Even though the rest of their school community knows about Kelcey, Tracey says she doesn't think they understand how dangerous measles would be for her. "Because she looks quite well, people might think she is out of danger, but if Kelcey got measles she could die."

"When I had Kelcey immunised as a preschooler, I did it to protect her and for the greater good. We need the majority of our population immunised to make it safer and healthier for everyone. I thought about the elderly and newborn babies, but it wasn't on my radar to think about kids with cancer."

"I know that people who choose not to immunise their children have their reasons and those reasons centre around doing the best thing for their child. I get that. The problem is that there are people in our community who do not have the luxury to choose whether to immunise or not. Kelcey cannot be immunised for anything because of her treatment, yet prior to her diagnosis she was fully immunised."

Kelcey is one of two children in the Roberts family. Her mum, dad and 7-year-old brother Maclain have all been immunised. Kelcey's immunisations no longer work because of the impact of chemotherapy on her immune system.

Although Kelcey hasn't been able to go to school for much of this year she has taken part in activities for kids living with cancer, and loves to email and skype with her friends.

What's the risk?

In the past, infectious diseases such as measles, mumps and rubella (MMR) caused many deaths. But vaccines can now prevent millions of deaths from such diseases.

Here you can see the chances of having a serious allergic reaction to the MMR vaccine compared to other risks we are exposed to almost every day.

What do you think about the dangers of getting vaccinated?

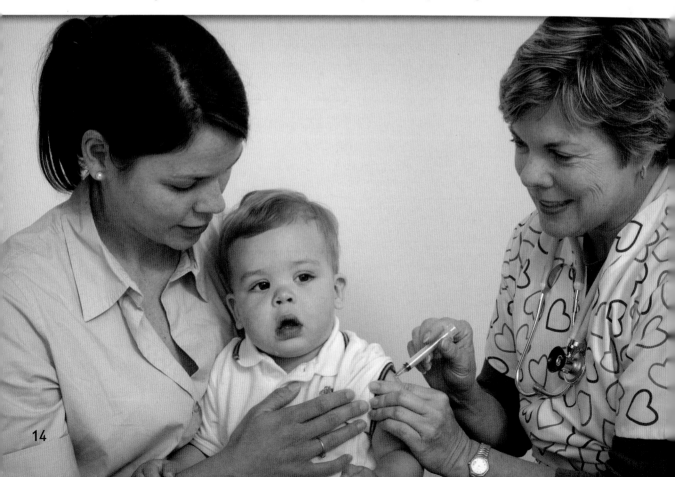

COMPARE THE RISK

Everything we do involves some kind of risk!

What are the chances ...

of dying in a motor vehicle accident?

139 deaths per 1,000,000 people

of dying from being unintentionally poisoned?

99 deaths per 1,000,000 people

of having a serious allergic reaction to the MMR vaccine?

less than 1 per 1,000,000 doses

The question of rights

Today, some parents are exercising their right not to have their children vaccinated against preventable diseases. Many are driven by concerns that the medicines designed to protect their children might have some side effects. To understand the issue, journalist Claire Halliday researched the facts and myths about vaccination and immunisation.

What are the risks from vaccination compared to the risks of catching measles?

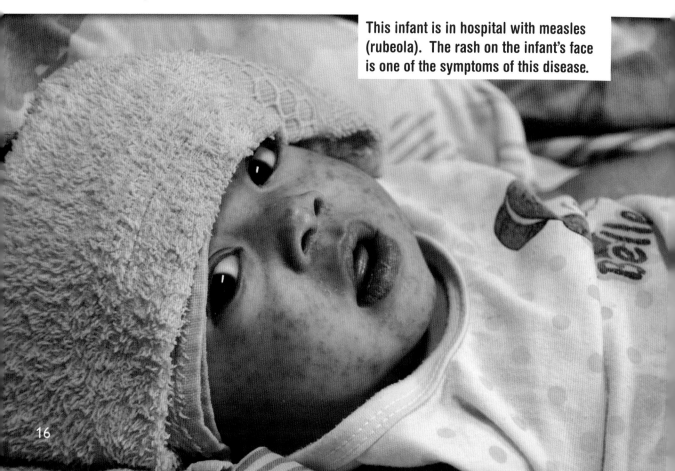

This infant is in hospital with measles (rubeola). The rash on the infant's face is one of the symptoms of this disease.

Vaccination – concerns

When you type the word "vaccination" or "immunisation" into the search engine of your computer, what pops up on your screen is a confusing mix of information – and there is no clear way to tell the difference between rumours and facts.

For a small number of children with serious health issues, it may be unwise for them to be vaccinated. Many respected doctors are clear that vaccinations for healthy children are lifesaving, but some people believe that vaccinations are bad for you – and have direct links to a range of health issues.

Vaccination – statistics

There is no doubt that childhood diseases, including measles and whooping cough (pertussis), are serious and can be fatal. The risk of complications caused by these diseases is much higher than the risks from immunisation. Some parents are alarmed by reports that link immunisation to disease complications, but when they choose to avoid vaccinations for their children, statistics show that the risks for their unprotected child are much more real.

Measles is a respiratory disease that starts with a fever, runny nose, cough, red eyes and sore throat. It can be deadly – especially in very young children. The risk of the measles, mumps, rubella (MMR) vaccine causing brain inflammation (encephalitis) is around one in one million. On the other hand, one in every 1000 children who catch measles will experience encephalitis. Of those affected children, one in ten will die and four in ten will suffer permanent brain damage.

Disease outbreak

When an outbreak of measles was linked to a theme park in late 2014, health officials recommended that all children under 12 months of age, as well as people who had never been immunised against the potentially deadly disease, should stay away.

Visitors to the theme park reported coming down with measles after visiting the park between 15 and 20 December 2014. Of the people infected by the outbreak, 82 per cent had not been vaccinated.

Very young children are at risk of becoming ill when there is an outbreak of a disease such as measles.

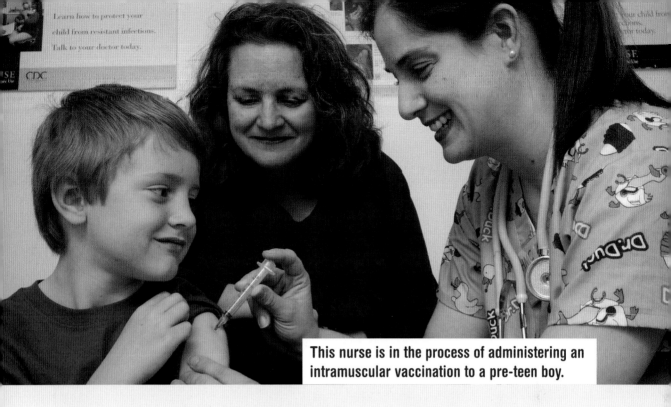

This nurse is in the process of administering an intramuscular vaccination to a pre-teen boy.

How you stay protected

When large percentages of a community are vaccinated, the whole community benefits. Even when between 80 and 85 per cent of people are vaccinated, the entire community can be protected because the risks of the disease being transmitted and spread are reduced.

This approach to immunisation protects all members of the community – including the 15 to 20 per cent who have not been immunised. This is called herd immunity.

In countries where immunisation rates are very high, many of the world's most deadly diseases have been virtually eliminated.

Receiving vaccinations against these preventable diseases when you are young means that you are protected. Although some people who are vaccinated can still catch the disease, it is never as serious as it is for people who have never been vaccinated.

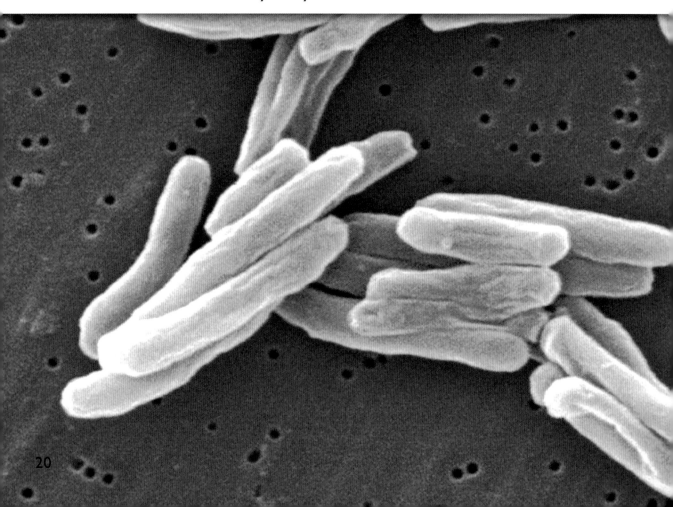

Going, going, gone!

Nineteenth-century doctors had to deal with a multitude of dreaded and highly contagious diseases.

Kathiann M. Kowalski describes some of the major illnesses of the 1800s and how they are treated today.

How many of these diseases have you heard about? If you have not heard of them, why do you think this is so?

Cholera is an infection that causes severe vomiting and diarrhoea. This disease is dangerous for infants and children. Thanks to clean drinking water, better sewerage systems and education about avoiding contaminated foods, cholera is rare in Australia, New Zealand, Europe and the United States today.

Consumption was a term used for what we now call tuberculosis. The bacteria could attack any part of the body, but usually affected the lungs. Transmitted person-to-person through the air, tuberculosis killed more people in Europe and North America than any other 19th-century disease.

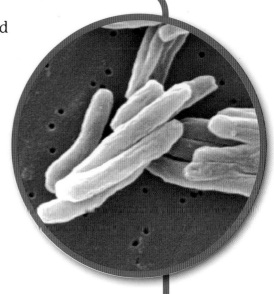

Today, most tuberculosis patients survive with antibiotics.

Diphtheria is a contagious bacterial disease. Its symptoms include swelling of the throat and mouth, which can make breathing impossible. It is spread by coughing and sneezing. But vaccination has made the illness rare in children today.

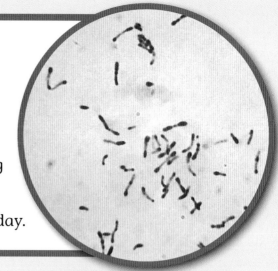

Measles, or rubeola, gets transmitted through the air. It causes a fever, runny nose and itchy rash, but these can develop into worse complications. Routine vaccination prevents measles for most children today.

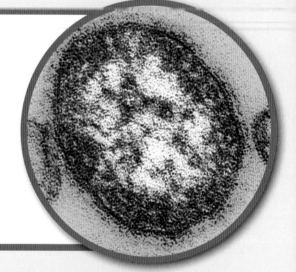

Pertussis, or whooping cough, is a highly contagious disease that gets passed along by the cough of an infected person. Vaccination is available to protect children from the disease today. Antibiotics are also used to treat it.

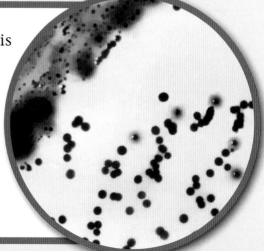

Rubella, or German measles, is a mild virus that shows itself as a rash on the face, trunk and limbs. It is transmitted through the air in droplets emitted through coughing or sneezing by an infected person. Today, the disease is rare because of vaccination.

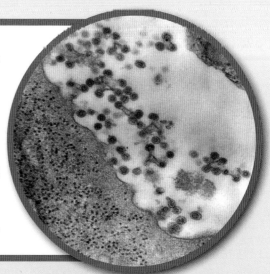

Scarlet fever causes a bright red rash, fever, chills, vomiting, sore throat and swollen glands. It is passed through germs found in the mouth and nasal fluids. If not treated with antibiotics, scarlet fever can infect the heart or kidneys.

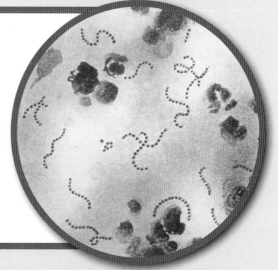

Typhoid fever results from eating contaminated food or drinking unclean water. Symptoms are fever, headache, coughing and rose-coloured spots on the skin. There is a vaccine for it. Otherwise, patients can take antibiotics.

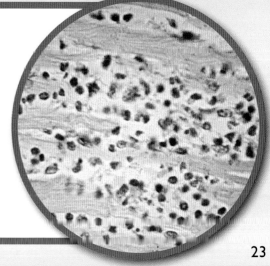

What is your opinion?: How to write a persuasive argument

1. State your opinion

Think about the issues related to your topic. What is your opinion?

2. Research

Research the information you need to support your opinion.

Related PERSPECTIVES book   Internet   Other sources

3. Make a plan

Introduction

How will you "hook" the reader?

State your opinion.

List reasons to support your opinion.

What persuasive devices will you use?

Reason 1
Support your reason
with evidence and details.

Reason 2
Support your reason
with evidence and details.

Reason 3
Support your reason
with evidence and details.

Conclusion

Restate your opinion. Leave your reader with a strong message.

4. Publish

Publish your persuasive argument.

Use visuals to reinforce your opinion.